I0796322

★★★★★

MLB TEAMS

Toronto BLUE JAYS

KENNY ABDO

Fly!
An Imprint of Abdo Zoom
abdobooks.com

abdobooks.com

Published by Abdo Zoom, a division of ABDO, P.O. Box 398166, Minneapolis, Minnesota 55439.

Printed in the United States of America, North Mankato, Minnesota.
102025
012026

Photo Credits: Bridgeman Images, Getty Images, Shutterstock
Production Contributors: Kenny Abdo, Jennie Forsberg, Grace Hansen
Design Contributors: Candice Keimig, Neil Klinepier

Library of Congress Control Number: 2025936815

Publisher's Cataloging-in-Publication Data

Names: Abdo, Kenny, author.
Title: Toronto Blue Jays / by Kenny Abdo
Description: Minneapolis, Minnesota : Abdo Zoom, 2026 | Series: MLB teams | Includes online resources and index.
Identifiers: ISBN 9798384940364 (lib. bdg.) | ISBN 9798384941125 (ebook) | ISBN 9798384941507 (read-to-me ebook)
Subjects: LCSH: Toronto Blue Jays (Baseball team)--Juvenile literature. | Baseball teams--Juvenile literature. | Professional sports--Juvenile literature. | Sports franchises--Juvenile literature. | Major League Baseball (Organization)--Juvenile literature.
Classification: DDC 796.357--dc23

Table of CONTENTS

BLUE JAYS

With swings as smooth as a blue jay's wings, Toronto's team soars and keeps the ballpark buzzing all season long!

BLUE

TD

From back-to-back titles to a history of Hall of Famers, the Jays fly high in Major League Baseball (MLB).

BATTER UP!

The Toronto Blue Jays began play in 1977 as Canada's second MLB team. The early years were tough, but the team slowly improved. In 1985, the Blue Jays won their first **division** title with 99 wins, the best **record** in the **American League** (**AL**) that year.

The Blue Jays were red hot in the late 1980s, nearly leading the **AL** with 215 home runs in 1987. With help from players like George Bell, the team made the playoffs in 1989. In 1991, the Jays led the league in attendance by drawing more than 4 million fans and returned to the playoffs.

BLUE
JAYS

In 1992, the Blue Jays made history by winning their first World Series! The Jays were the first MLB team outside the United States to claim a ring. Roberto Alomar and Joe Carter led the offense while Jack Morris pitched heat. Pat Borders hit .450 to win MVP.

GRAND SLAMS

Amazingly, the Blue Jays won the 1993 World Series against the Phillies. Joe Carter hit a **walk-off** home run in Game 6. It is still one of the most famous plays in baseball history.

The team had a strong lineup with Paul Molitor and John Olerud. Toronto had become a baseball powerhouse.

19

After the success of the 1990s, the Blue Jays missed the playoffs for more than 20 years. However, they still found ways to win. They simply hit the ball over the fence, over and over again. The Blue Jays hit 257 home runs in 2010 and won 85 games. Despite their strong play, the **AL** East was tough to go up against.

The team finally broke through, appearing in the **AL** Championship Series in 2015 and 2016. In 2021, Vladimir Guerrero Jr. tied for most home runs with 48. Alek Manoah had a 3.22 **ERA** and struck out 127 batters.

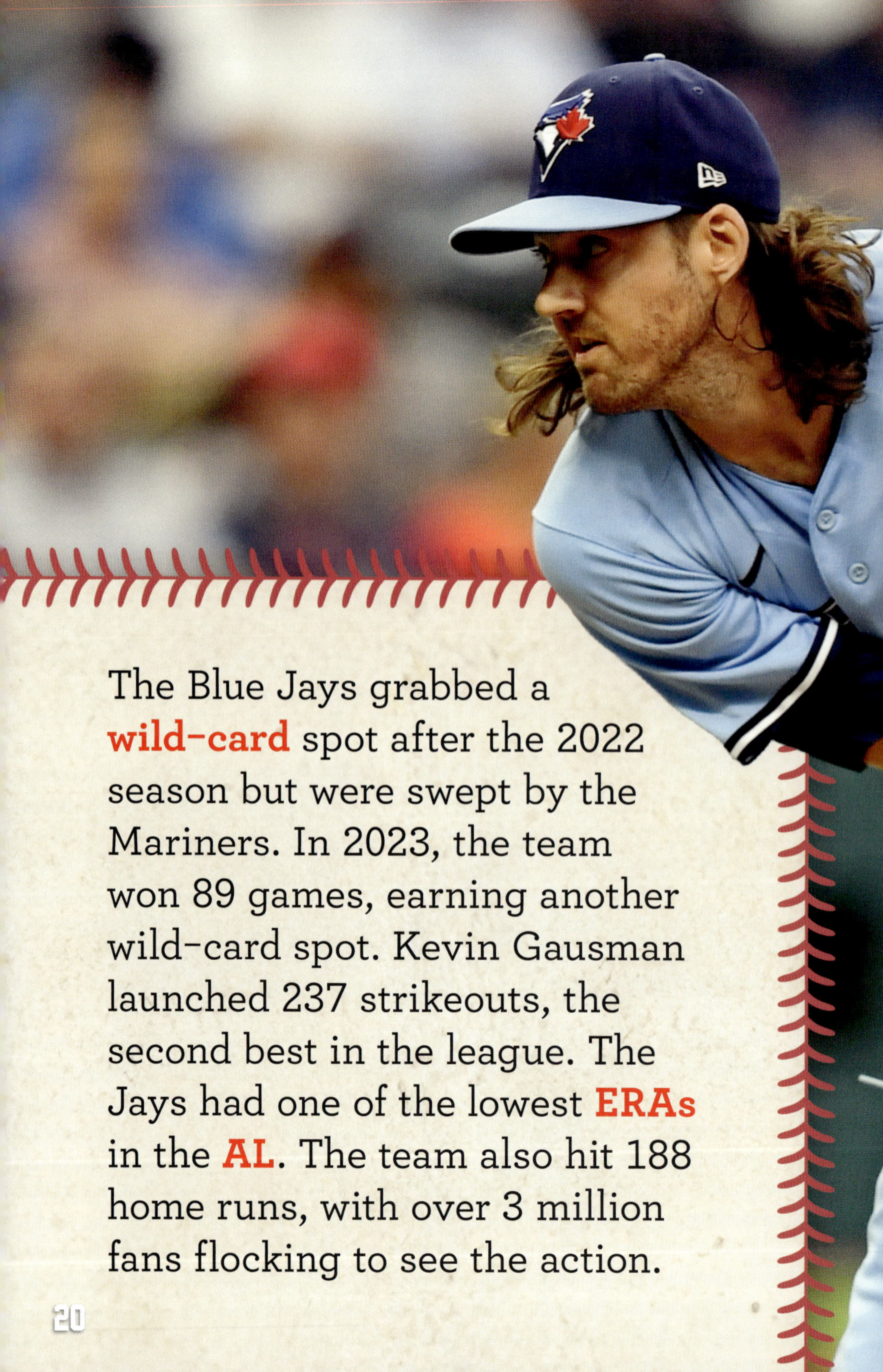

The Blue Jays grabbed a **wild-card** spot after the 2022 season but were swept by the Mariners. In 2023, the team won 89 games, earning another wild-card spot. Kevin Gausman launched 237 strikeouts, the second best in the league. The Jays had one of the lowest **ERAs** in the **AL**. The team also hit 188 home runs, with over 3 million fans flocking to see the action.

AYS

In 2025, the Blue Jays took first place in the **AL** East with a 94–68 **record**. They won the AL **Division** Series and Championship Series to go all the way to the Fall Classic. Guerrero stood out in the World Series, hitting a homer in Games 4 and 5. The Jays played well and it looked like they might win it all. But they ultimately lost to the Dodgers in Game 7. Even with the heartbreaking loss, the 2025 Blue Jays would be remembered for years to come.

HALL OF FAME

Joe Carter hit 203 home runs as a Blue Jay and helped the team win back-to-back World Series titles. In 1991, he hit 33 home runs and had 108 **RBIs**. Carter became a legend by hitting a **walk-off** home run to win the 1993 World Series. In 2003, he was named to the Canadian Baseball Hall of Fame.

TORONTO

Second baseman Roberto Alomar made five **All-Star** teams and won five **Gold Gloves** during his time with the Blue Jays. In 1993, he batted .326 and stole 55 bases. Alomar helped the team win two World Series titles and was named to the Baseball Hall of Fame in 2011.

ROBERTO ALOMAR VELAZQUEZ
"ROBBIE"
SAN DIEGO, N.L., 1988-90; TORONTO, A.L., 1991-95;
BALTIMORE, A.L., 1996-98; CLEVELAND, A.L., 1999-2001;
NEW YORK, N.L., 2002-03; CHICAGO, A.L., 2003-04;
ARIZONA, N.L., 2004
SET THE STANDARD FOR A GENERATION OF SECOND BASEMEN WITH A QUICK, POWERFUL BAT, A SMOOTH, STEADY GLOVE AND SEEMINGLY ENDLESS RANGE. MEMBER OF A PUERTO RICAN FAMILY OF BASEBALL STARS, HIS GRACE, TIRELESS PREPARATION AND POISED PRESENCE RESULTED IN A .300 BATTING AVERAGE, 2,724 HITS, 210 HOME RUNS, 474 STOLEN BASES, AND 12 ALL-STAR GAME APPEARANCES. HIS 10 GOLD GLOVE AWARDS ARE A POSITION RECORD. A MODEL OF CONSISTENCY, HIT .300 OR BETTER NINE TIMES. SPURRED BLUE JAYS TO CONSECUTIVE WORLD SERIES TITLES IN 1992-1993.

Toronto

Roy Halladay was one of the best pitchers in Blue Jays history. He won the **Cy Young Award** in 2003 and threw more than 2,000 strikeouts in his career. Halladay made six **All-Star** teams with the Jays and led the **AL** in complete games five times. He entered the Baseball Hall of Fame in 2019.

GLOSSARY

All-Star – a team consisting of athletes chosen as the best at their positions from all teams in a league or region.

American League (AL) – one of two 15-team leagues that make up MLB.

Cy Young Award – an annual American baseball award given to the best pitcher in each of the two MLB leagues.

division – a number of teams grouped together in a sport for competitive purposes.

Earned-Run Average (ERA) – the average number of earned runs per game scored against a pitcher.

Gold Glove – an annual award given to the best fielders at each position in both the AL and National League (NL).

record – a team's season total of wins and losses.

Runs Batted In (RBI) – a statistic that credits a batter for making a play that allows a run to be scored.

walk-off – any victory in which the home team scores the winning run in the bottom of the final inning.

wild-card – a place or a team chosen to fill a place in a competition after the regularly qualified players or teams have all been decided.

ONLINE RESOURCES

To learn more about the Toronto Blue Jays, please visit **abdobooklinks.com** or scan this QR code. These links are routinely monitored and updated to provide the most current information available.

INDEX